Raptors

By Jill Atkins

Published in 2026 by
Norwood House Press
2544 Clinton Street
Buffalo, NY 14224

Copyright © Ransom Publishing Ltd.
Text copyright © Ransom Publishing Ltd.
Photographs copyright © iStock.com/Liene Helmig; Nastasic; Jjacob; wrangel; MelanieMaya; Wirestock; BrianEKushner; Wildpix645; GarysFRP; Christopher Hall; Sunan Wongsa-nga; Henk Bogaard; Steve Midgley; nieudacza; CarolinaBirdman; Jeff Huth; meadowmouse; lavin photography; Steve Adams; Edwin Tan.
Illustrations copyright © Aleksandar Sotirovski
Photographs copyright © iStock.com/serts; AlbyDeTweede; Knaupe; JMrocek; Hanne Kobaek; keiichihiki; JasonOndreicka; Antrey; Chris Rogers; alexandrumagurean; Darren Curzon; ilbusca; RockingStock; Rafael_Wiedenmeier; teddyandmia; BalazsKovacs; Alphotographic; grahamheywood; Smileus; cunfek; digital_eye.
All rights reserved. No part of this book may be reproduced in any form without permission in writing from the publisher, except by a reviewer.

Printed in the United States of America

Library of Congress Cataloging-in-Publication Data:
Names: Atkins, Jill (Children's author). | Jones, Cath, 1965-, author. | Sotirovski, Aleksandar, illustrator.
Title: Raptors / written by Jill Atkins. The big chop / written by Cath Jones, illustrated by Aleksandar Sotirovski. I'm a beech tree / written by Jill Atkins.
Description: Buffalo, NY : Norwood House Press, 2026. | Series: Phonics all-stars: phase 5a
Identifiers: ISBN 9781978578890 (pbk.) | ISBN 9781978578906 (library bound) | ISBN 9781978578913 (ebook)
Subjects: LCSH: Reading–Phonetic method–Juvenile fiction. | English language–Phonetics–Juvenile fiction. | Birds of prey–Juvenile fiction. | Baldness–Juvenile fiction. | Beech–Juvenile fiction.
Classification: LCC LB1573.3 A796 | DDC 372.465–dc23

CPSIA compliance information: Batch #CW26NHP: For further information contact Norwood House Press at 1-800-237-9932.

Raptors are birds that hunt and kill for food.

Raptors enjoy floating on currents of air as they look for food.

This is a **condor**. It is a big bird, with a wingspan of up to ten feet.

Raptors have much better sight than people.

From high up, a raptor can pinpoint the exact spot its dinner is lurking.

When it spots something, it swoops down to grab it.

Raptors hunt for little mammals such as rats, as well as frogs, toads, insects, and little birds. Some bigger raptors hunt for rabbits, squirrels, and fish too.

This raptor is standing on something bigger than that!

Raptors have strong, sharp talons to grip the food.

The raptors' bills are like sharp hooks for ripping the animal.

When raptors have chicks, the mom and dad will bring food back to the nest.

At first, they snip off little bits of the animal and feed it to the chicks. Then the chicks start to rip off bits of the food with no help from the mom or dad.

The **buzzard** is a common sort of raptor.

Buzzards can often be seen high up near trees. They like habitats like woodland or farmland.

Girl

Boy

Girl buzzards are bigger than boys.

Some raptors are little. The **kestrel** is one of the little raptors. It is not much bigger than a blackbird.

In the air it is so quick, it looks like a dart.

Kestrels often hover near main roads, but they can be seen on farmland and in towns too.

Owls are raptors. They hunt at dusk or at night. You might hear an owl hooting in the night.

This little owl has a rat in its talons. It will polish it off all in one go.

Raptors are so good at hunting that the Kazak people train them, to help them hunt for food.

The Big Chop

Written by
Cath Jones

Illustrated by
Aleksandar Sotirovski

Sue was living in a trailer park. She had been living there with her mom for three years.

This morning, when Sue had left the trailer, she had felt restless and a bit blue. She didn't like to argue with her mom.

There was a boy sitting on a bench at the end of the avenue, next to the shop.

He had short hair – or was it no hair? That was odd.

Sue hid, so he did not see her.

The next morning, Sue went to the shop to get some soap.

The boy with the short hair was there.

He didn't see Sue.

Sue didn't like the look of him, so she just got the soap and left.

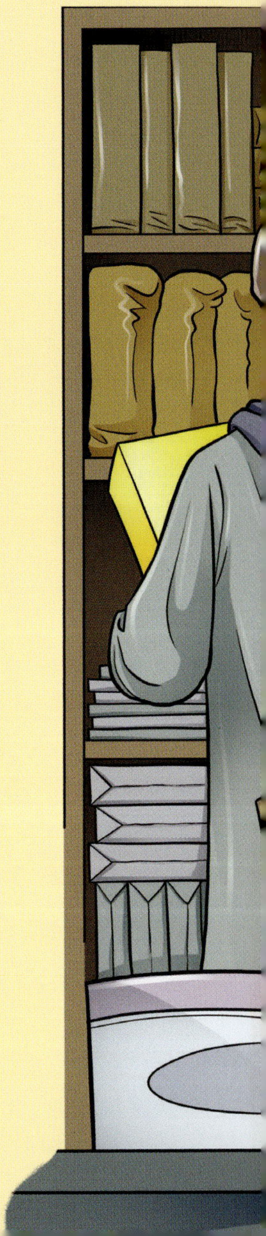

The next morning, the boy with the short hair was sitting on a bench.

He was with a man.

"That's Faheem and his dad," a man said to Sue. "Faheem is a good boy."

Sue felt herself blush.

The next week, Sue met Faheem in the avenue.

"In the shop – did you see my short hair and then rush out?" Faheem said with a grin.

Sue felt herself going a bit pink.

"Lots of people do that when they see me," Faheem went on. "You see, I had long hair, just like you. Then my mom cut it all off!"

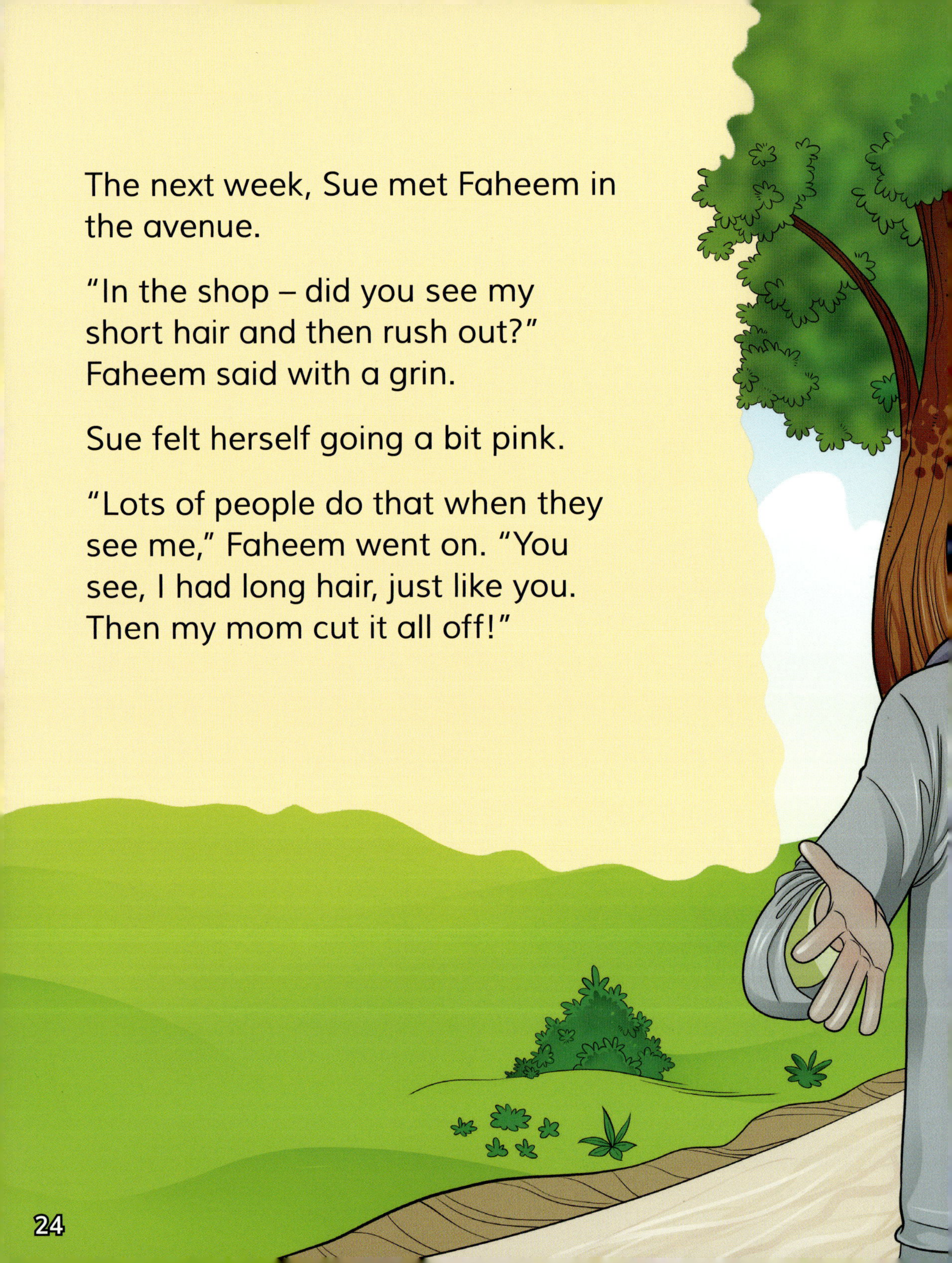

"It was all in aid of Dad," Faheem said. "There were loads of people there. Mom had her clippers and I got a buzz cut! We were given loads of cash."

Faheem bent down and
Sue felt his hair.

It was so short! It felt odd.

"Dad's got a long illness. He needs lots of drugs to help him get better," Faheem said. "The drugs cost a lot, so we help to get the cash for them."

"That's so sad," said Sue. "How can I help?"

"Come with me now," said Faheem. "We are all meeting up in the club. Dad will be there."

Faheem took Sue to the club to meet his dad.

When Sue went into the venue, loads of people were clapping.

Sue sat down in the barber's chair.

"I'm so glad I can help," she said.

Faheem's mom held the clippers tight, as
Sue's long hair fell onto the arm of the chair.

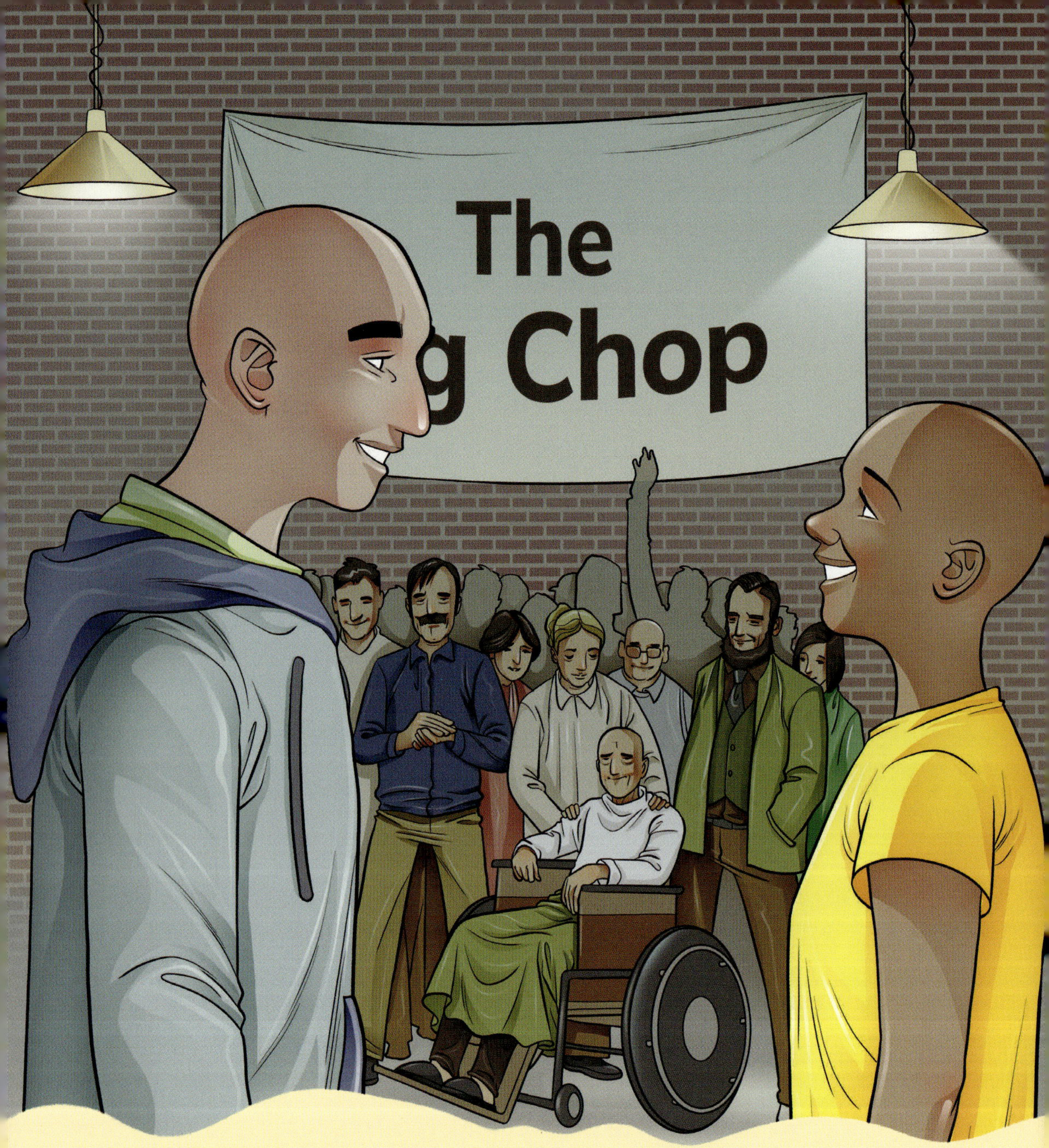

"I'm so glad I can help get some cash for Dad.
Now I look just like you!" Sue said with a big grin.

I'm a Beech Tree

By Jill Atkins

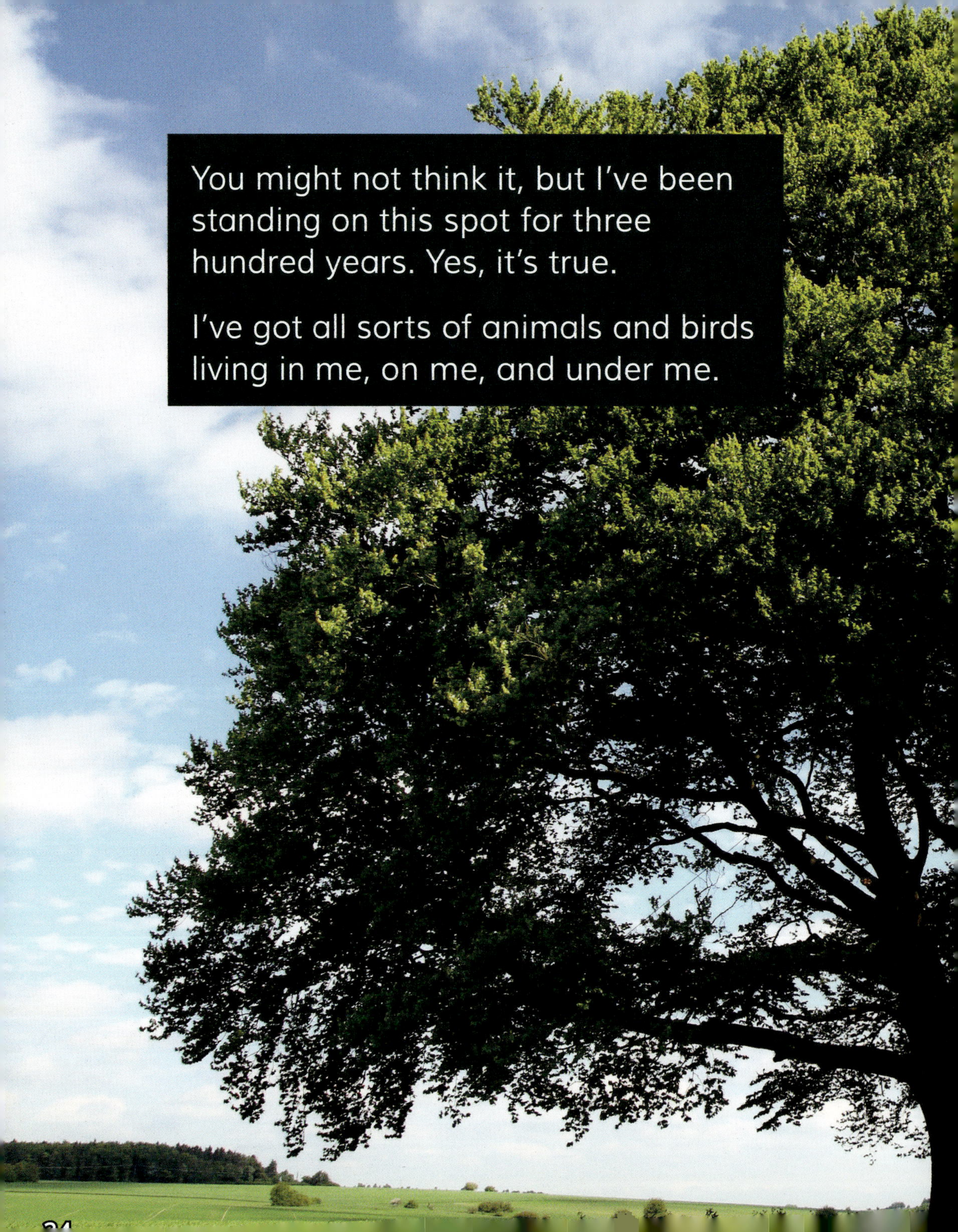

You might not think it, but I've been standing on this spot for three hundred years. Yes, it's true.

I've got all sorts of animals and birds living in me, on me, and under me.

There are foxes living under my roots, a woodpecker is nesting in my trunk, and crows are nesting right at the top.

Insects are dashing up and down my smooth bark, but it can be hard to see them.

I can often see a squirrel gathering beechnuts, and at night I can hear an owl hooting.

I have seen so much in all the years I've been living in this spot.

At first, people traveled on foot or with a cart.

Then people dug canals for long boats.

Then they laid rails for monster trains that puffed along.

Roads were laid too, and cars were invented.

Towns got much bigger and the air started to turn black.

That was not so good. For the animals and me, it was hard to keep going.

Standing in this spot, I have seen it all.

I have seen a girl and a boy meet at my trunk. They cut something into my bark. (That was not a good thing to do!)

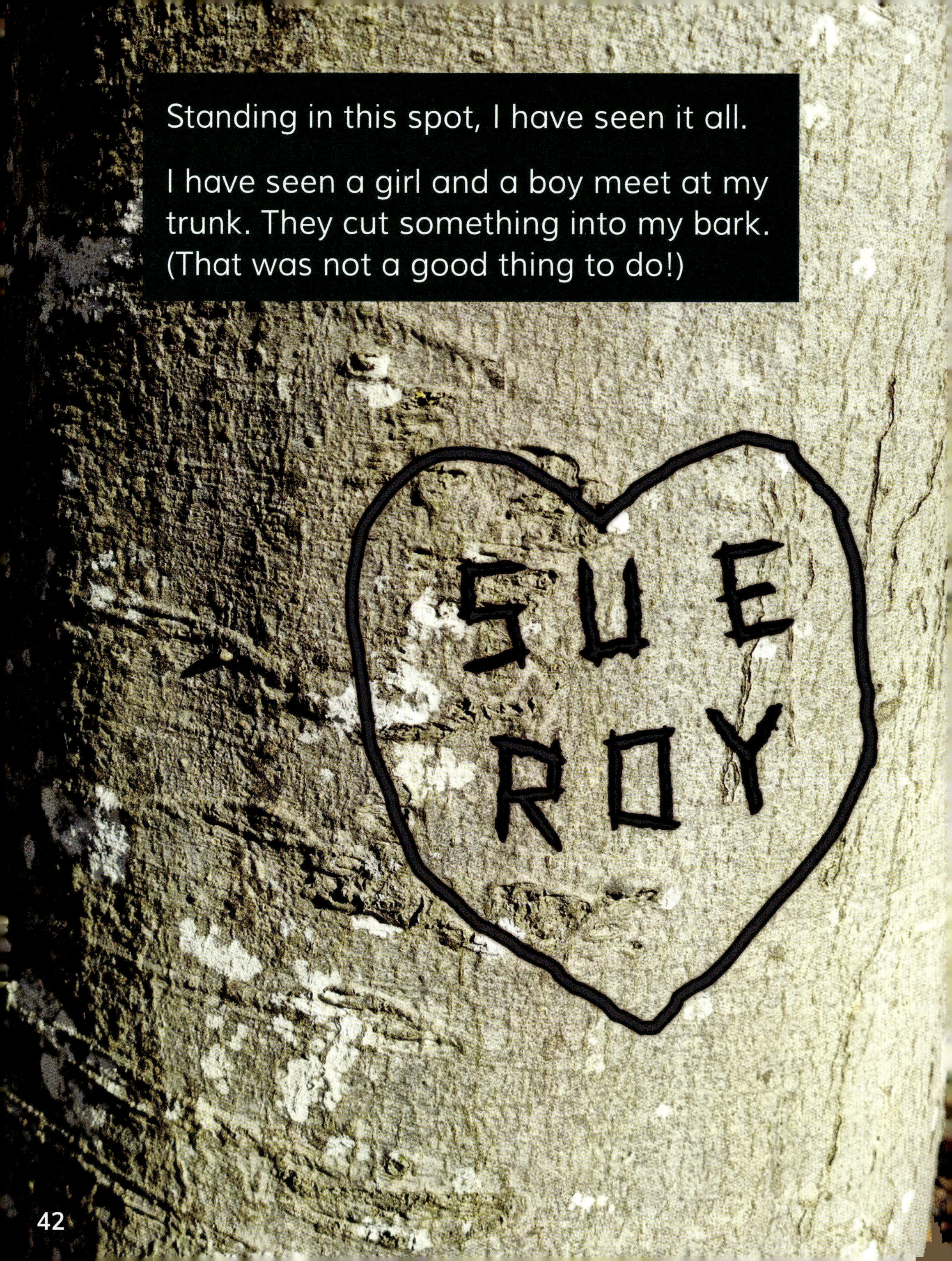

I've had people standing under me, sheltering from storms.

They tell you not to do that. If lightning struck me, you might get a shock. (So far, thank goodness, that hasn't happened!)

Back when I was a little tree, there was a big fight next to me.

The first crowd of men ran into the forest. Then a second lot pursued them. They argued, then they started fighting.

It was such a racket, with the clash of steel and the yelling.

The best part of the year is when my green turns to a stunning brown hue.

Then I start waiting for winter to set in.

Winter is hard for a lot of animals, but it is when I can get a good rest.

We're good, us beech trees.

I intend to enjoy this spot for years and years. What sorts of things will I see in the years to come?